ALOHA! Scott Hanft 2005

KAUA'I EDGE
A PHOTOGRAPHIC PORTFOLIO

Steve Alterman and Scott Hanft

OUTER BANKS PRESS | publisher

KAUA'I EDGE
A Photographic Portfolio
Steve Alterman & Scott Hanft

Published in 2003 by Outer Banks Press, a subsidiary of OBBC, Inc.

ISBN: 0-9713890-2-0

Library of Congress Cataloging-in-Publication data available by request

EDITOR: Linda L. Lauby
DESIGN: Sara Birkemeier and George Scott, 8 DOT Graphics WWW.8DOTGRAPHICS.COM

Printed in China

This book was created using QuarkXPress 4.1 and Adobe Photoshop 6.0 on a Macintosh G4.
The text is set in Adobe Garamond and Helvetica Neue.

Cover photos: Steve Alterman & Scott Hanft

FOR BULK PURCHASES, SPECIAL SALES AND LIMITED EDITION PRINTS, PLEASE CONTACT:
Outer Banks Press
Post Office Box 2829
Kitty Hawk, North Carolina 27949
252.261.0612
252.261.0613 fax
WWW.OUTERBANKSPRESS.COM
MAIL@OUTERBANKSPRESS.COM

TABLE OF CONTENTS

PLUMERIA BLOSSOMS
[Scott Hanft]

5

On September 11, 1992, Hurricane Iniki tore

through the island of Kaua'i. Debris flew through

the air, mature trees were uprooted, roofs were

torn off virtually every building and hotels

were destroyed. When the hurricane passed,

Kaua'i was quite simply in shambles.

The island's comeback to its former beauty is

directly attributable to the resilience of the land

and the people. It is to this "Spirit of Kaua'i"

that this volume is dedicated.

THE FURY OF HURRICANE INIKI, SEPTEMBER 11, 1992
[Scott Hanft]

INTRODUCTION

The Island of Kaua'i is the oldest and "greenest" of the major Hawaiian Islands. It lies only 103 miles north and west of the island of Oahu and the city of Honolulu, but in spirit it is worlds apart. Nicknamed "The Garden Isle," it offers a glimpse of just how lovely an island can be.

Almost round in shape, Kaua'i is a land of contrasts. Fed by the runoff from Mount Wai'ale'ale (the wettest spot on earth, which receives more than 480 annual inches of rain), Kaua'i's north shore is a lush paradise of streams, waterfalls, rainbows, and checkerboard patterns of the many taro fields in and around the picturesque town of Hanalei. It also is home to some of the most beautiful beaches found anywhere. The south shore, on the other hand, consists of a dry, desert-like, environment, with perpetual sun and very little rainfall. Many of the island's resorts are located along this coast, especially in the Poipu Beach area. But resorts are not the only attraction of this side of Kaua'i: the lithified sand dunes of the Maha'ulepu coast provide an unusual attractive landscape; Spouting Horn's blowhole sends seawater skyward on a regular basis; and the town of Waimea is the jumping-off point for excursions into Waimea Canyon and Koke'e State Park. Waimea overlooks the spectacular Na Pali coast, where dolphins and whales play offshore. The Alaka'i Swamp, which has perhaps the highest elevation of any swamp in the world, is also accessible from this area. The Na Pali coast itself is inaccessible to automobiles and must be visited on foot, by boat or from the air. For the hardy, the 11-mile Kalalau Trail connects Ke'e Beach to the north with the Kalalau Valley to the south.

Kaua'i is, quite simply, a photographer's paradise. The varied landscape and its vibrant colors provide a palette that is irresistible. *Kaua'i Edge* represents the work of two award-winning photographers from wildly different backgrounds, both of whom have fallen in love with the island. They met by chance at the Kaua'i Products Fair in January 2001 and a year later decided to collaborate on this volume. Scott Hanft is based on Kaua'i, while Steve Alterman lives on the East Coast of the United States and uses annual "business trips" to Hawai'i as an excuse to explore the island. Both appreciate and revere the island; this book is their attempt to convey the beauty of this unique land.

In terms of structure, *Kaua'i Edge* is a clockwise tour of the island, beginning in the Hanakapi'ai Valley and ending with a view of the Na Pali coast. "Side trips" away from the coast into the interior are made whenever photographic opportunities appear. *Aloha!*

LEI ON TUNNELS BEACH
Modern legend holds that if a visitor throws a lei out to the waves, he or she will return if the lei is washed back onto the shore. [Steve Alterman]

Hanakapi'ai Falls
[Scott Hanft]

Hanakapi'ai Stream
[Steve Alterman]

BACKGROUND: Fern on Hanakapi'ai Trail. [Steve Alterman]

KALALAU TRAIL BETWEEN KE'E BEACH AND HANAKAPI'AI
[Scott Hanft]

KE'E BEACH
Rainbow off the Na Pali Cliffs [Scott Hanft]
Sunset on the Na Pali Cliffs [Steve Alterman]

WINTER WAVES AT KEʻE BEACH
[Steve Alterman]

The mood of Kauaʻi's beaches changes

dramatically with the seasons. At Keʻe Beach,

summer brings calm seas and great snorkeling.

Winter, on the other hand, sees wild surf

crashing on the beach and the nearby rocks.

KEʻE BEACH SUNSET
[Scott Hanft]

Convict Tangs with Surgeon Fish
[Scott Hanft]

Humuhumu nukunuku apaʻa (Triggerfish)
Hawaiʻi's State Fish [Scott Hanft]

Underwater at Keʻe Beach
[Scott Hanft]

Green Sea Turtle, or Honu, Tunnels Beach
[Scott Hanft]

WAIKANALOA WET CAVE ON THE NORTH SHORE AT HAʻENA
[Steve Alterman]

The runoff from Mount Waiʻaleʻale feeds

hundreds of streams and waterfalls around the

island. On its way to the Pacific Ocean,

Limahuli Stream passes through a tropical

botanical garden.

LIMAHULI STREAM
[Steve Alterman]

TUNNELS BEACH FROM THE AIR
[Scott Hanft]

MORNING AT TUNNELS BEACH
[Steve Alterman]

BACKGROUND: Morning Glories on the Beach [Steve Alterman]

Tunnels Beach is a favorite haunt for

snorkelers and surfers. Anchored on the

west by Makana Peak ("Bali Hai" of

South Pacific fame), the beach is one of the

most picturesque on the island.

TUNNELS BEACH
End of the Day [Steve Alterman]

34

HIGH SURF AT TUNNELS
[Steve Alterman]

WAINIHA SUNRISE
[Steve Alterman]

LUMAHA'I BEACH
Lumaha'i Stream Entering the Ocean [Steve Alterman]

BRAZILIAN CARDINAL
An introduced species, the Brazilian Cardinal now thrives all over Kaua'i. [Steve Alterman]

LUMAHAʻI BEACH AND HANALEI BAY FROM THE AIR
[Scott Hanft]

LUMAHAʻI BEACH
[Scott Hanft]

WINTER STORM AT LUMAHA'I BEACH
[Steve Alterman]

CHAMELEON PORTRAIT
[Scott Hanft]

ALAKAʻI RIDGE FROM THE AIR
[Scott Hanft]

STORM IN THE MOUNTAINS BEHIND HANALEI
[Scott Hanft]

MOUNTAIN DETAIL BEHIND HANALEI
[Scott Hanft]

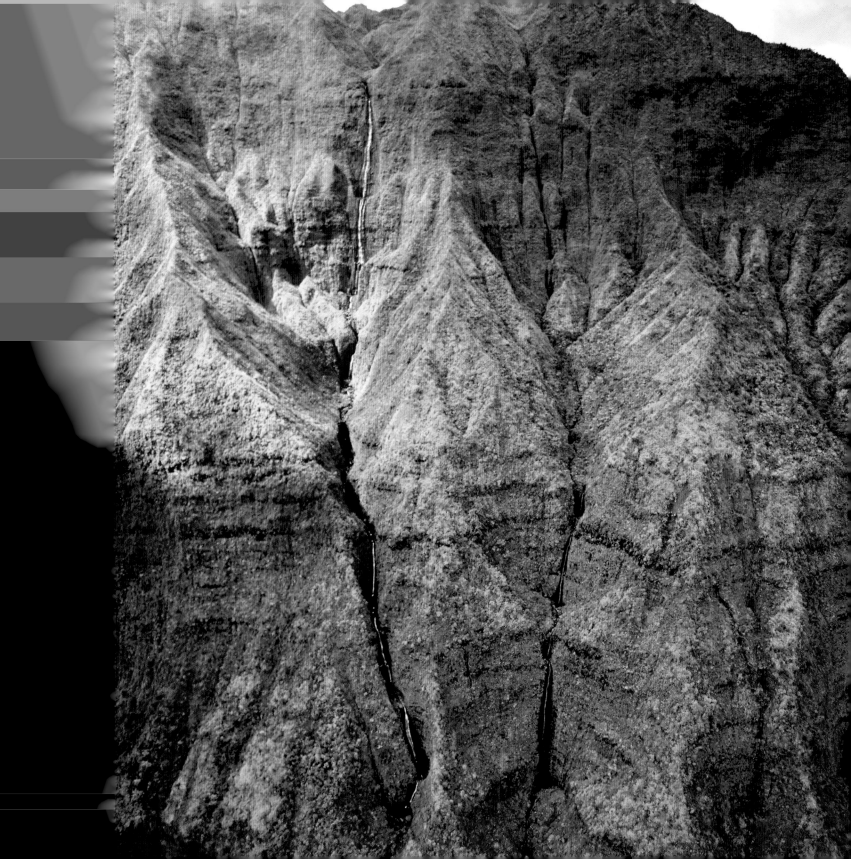

Hanalei Bay, with its miles-long fringe of

beach, is home to sailors, surfers and

sunbathers. Occupying the bay's

perimeter, the town of Hanalei is the

hub for north shore activities.

Hanalei Bay Sunset
[Scott Hanft]

"Rainbow Sky" at Hanalei Bay
[Scott Hanft]

Hanalei Pier
[Scott Hanft]

WAIʻOLI CHURCH, HANALEI
[Scott Hanft]

HANALEI OVERLOOK
Hanalei's taro fields supply much of the state's taro, the root used to make
poi, a Hawaiian dietary staple. [Steve Alterman]

MATURE TARO PLANTS, HANALEI
[Scott Hanft]

Background: Taro Fields [Steve Alterman]

 **TARO FIELDS, HANALEI**
[Steve Alterman]

HANALEI TARO FIELDS
[Steve Alterman]

HANALEI REFLECTIONS
[Steve Alterman]

62

The planned community of Princeville sits on

a peninsula that juts out into the Pacific on

Kaua'i's north shore. It is home to the natural

swimming hole known as Queen's Bath, plus

numerous albatross and spectacular sunsets.

PRINCEVILLE SUNSET
[Steve Alterman]

PRINCEVILLE RAINBOW
[Steve Alterman]

PINK SKY, PRINCEVILLE
[Steve Alterman]

THE MOODS OF PRINCEVILLE
[Steve Alterman]

Morning at Queen's Bath, Princeville
[Steve Alterman]

PAINTED BARK EUCALYPTUS
[Steve Alterman, left; Scott Hanft, right]

The surf at north shore's Kalihiwai Beach

can be spectacular, and is often a

challenge to even the most experienced

surfers and windsurfers.

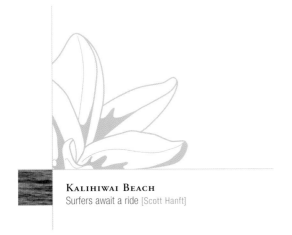

KALIHIWAI BEACH
Surfers await a ride [Scott Hanft]

KALIHIWAI BEACH
A Lone Surfer Waits for the Perfect Wave [Scott Hanft]

WEST COAST WINDSURFING ACTION
[Scott Hanft]

With Kilauea Lighthouse in the

distance, the view from the usually

deserted ʻAnini Beach provides a

colorful and quiet start to any day.

ʻANINI SUNRISE
[Steve Alterman]

First Light at 'Anini Beach
[Steve Alterman]

PLUMERIA BLOSSOMS
[Steve Alterman]

UNNAMED WATERFALL ALONG THE ROAD IN KILAUEA
[Steve Alterman]

KILAUEA LIGHTHOUSE
[Steve Alterman]

NESTING ALBATROSS
[Steve Alterman]

KILAUEA POINT FROM SECRET BEACH
[Steve Alterman]

CLAMSHELL LENS IN KILAUEA LIGHTHOUSE
[Scott Hanft]

KILAUEA POINT
Evening Flight [Scott Hanft]

CHRIST MEMORIAL EPISCOPAL CHURCH, KILAUEA
[Scott Hanft]

Christ Memorial Episcopal Church, Kilauea
[Scott Hanft]

BACKGROUND: Plumerias [Steve Alterman]

O'AHU IN THE DISTANCE, FROM KEALIA BEACH
[Scott Hanft]

WAILUA RESERVOIR
[Steve Alterman, left; Scott Hanft, above]

FERN GROTTO, WAILUA
[Steve Alterman]

'OPEAKA'A FALLS
A Rare View from the Bottom of the Falls [Scott Hanft]

WAILUA FALLS
[Steve Alterman]

WAILUA FALLS
[Scott Hanft]

KIPU FALLS, SOUTH SHORE
[Steve Alterman]

BACKGROUND: Kipu Falls Detail [Steve Alterman]

Past Poipu Beach's luxury hotels, through

the cane fields, and on the coastline,

lie the lithified sand dunes of

Maha'ulepu. Punctuated by pocket

beaches and weird, fantastic formations,

this landscape bears little resemblance

to any other part of the island.

MAHA'ULEPU COAST, SOUTH SHORE
[Steve Alterman]

MAHA'ULEPU COAST, SOUTH SHORE
[Steve Alterman]

OLD CHURCH WINDOW, KOLOA AND KOLOA CHURCH

[Scott Hanft]

SPOUTING HORN AT SUNSET
[Steve Alterman]

National Tropical Botanical Gardens, Lawaʻi
[Scott Hanft]

OLD MARKET, HANAPEPE
[Scott Hanft]

WAIMEA CANYON VIEWS

One of Kaua'i's major geologic features is Waimea Canyon, a colorful 10-mile gash in the island's southeast corner. It is home to the 'iliau plant (left), a native species found nowhere else, as well as numerous waterfalls and unusual rock formations.

[Steve Alterman, left and above right; Scott Hanft, above left]

HAWAIIAN BARN OWL SOARING OVER KOKE‘E
[Scott Hanft]

CLEARING STORM IN WAIMEA CANYON
[Steve Alterman]

SMALL WATERFALL IN WAIMEA CANYON
[Steve Alterman]

TOP OF WAIPO'O FALLS, WAIMEA CANYON
[Steve Alterman]

SECLUDED WATERFALL, MOUNT WAIʻALEʻALE
[Scott Hanft]

ALAKAʻI SWAMP, MOUNT WAIʻALEʻALE
[Scott Hanft]

BACKGROUND: Lehua Blossom [Steve Alterman]

LEHUA BLOSSOMS, ALAKAʻI SWAMP
[Scott Hanft]

INSIDE MOUNT WAIʻALEʻALE
[Steve Alterman]

Na Pali Coast from the Air
[Scott Hanft]

Awaʻawapuhi Overlook, Na Pali Coast
[Steve Alterman]

Kalalau Valley from the Pihea Trail
[Steve Alterman]

West Side Sunset with Niʻihau in the Distance
[Scott Hanft]

Mist Along the Na Pali Coast
[Scott Hanft]

Na Pali Coast Rainbow
[Scott Hanft]

Bird of Paradise
[Steve Alterman]

Kaua'i's Na Pali coast stretches more than 11 miles along the island's west side, and is nearly is inaccessible. Erosion over millions of years has sculpted the landscape into an other-worldly array of spires and valleys.

Na Pali Spires
[Scott Hanft]

BREACHING HUMPBACK WHALES
[Scott Hanft]

YOUNG SPINNER DOLPHIN AT PLAY
[Scott Hanft]

DOLPHIN POD
[Scott Hanft]

East Side Cane Road
[Scott Hanft]

ACKNOWLEDGMENTS

I never thought I would ask a publisher located in Kitty Hawk, North Carolina to assist with a book depicting the Island of Kaua'i. When I did, however, Linda Lauby of Outer Banks Press was there with her help. Without her, we could never have published this volume. The graphic design was done by Sara Birkemeier and George Scott of 8 Dot Graphics in Raleigh, North Carolina; to a very large extent, the beauty of the book is directly attributable to their work.

I would also like to thank my wife, Lynne, for letting me schlep all my camera gear on our annual trips to Hawai'i and for not complaining when I arise before dawn (waking everyone up in the process) to shoot at sunrise. And thanks to Doug and Annell Kuelpman, the world's best friends, for accompanying us on these annual adventures.

On Kaua'i, Nancy Young of the Kahn Gallery in Hanalei has been a constant source of encouragement and inspiration. And, of course, I would like to thank Scott Hanft for sharing his images and agreeing to become part of this project.

Steve Alterman

I would like to thank my parents for all their support and education they have provided over the years. I also thank John Gray, my photography teacher during my years attending Moorpark Junior College. He had a key role in providing influence and inspiration in my style of photography. In addition, special thanks go to the California Institute of the Arts for surrounding me with the world of art and conferring upon me a bachelor's degree in fine art photography. My photography teachers, John Divola, John Bach, Jo Ann Callis and Allen Sekula, were instrumental in the mentoring process and, through their great talents, for providing the inspiration for me to make photography a full-time profession.

I would also like to thank the owners, captains and crew at Na Pali Eco Adventures. The job as a captain there gave me the means to survive on Kaua'i and to get 11 years' worth of beautiful photo opportunities of marine life and Na Pali coast scenery from an offshore perspective.

Scott Hanft

THE VIEW FROM HIDEAWAYS BEACH, PRINCEVILLE
[Steve Alterman]

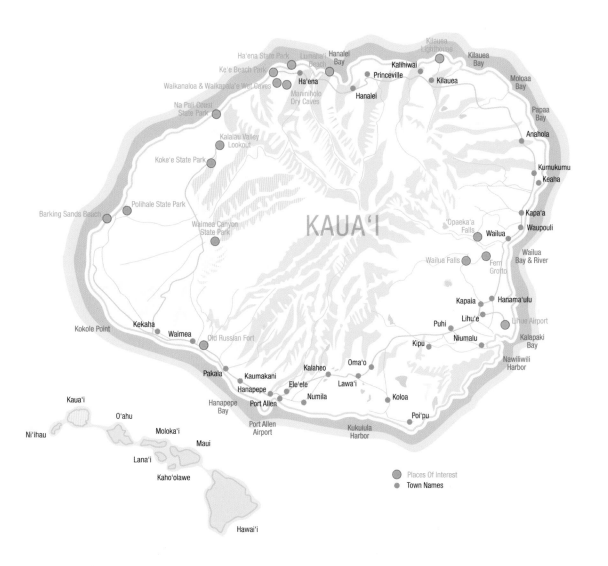

KAUA'I

Ha'ena State Park
Lumaha'i Beach
Hanalei Bay
Kilauea Lighthouse
Kilauea Bay
Ke'e Beach Park
Kalihiwai
Waikanaloa & Waikapala'e Wet Caves
Ha'ena
Princeville
Kilauea
Moloaa Bay
Maniniholo Dry Caves
Hanalei
Papaa Bay
Na Pali Coast State Park
Anahola
Kalalau Valley Lookout
Kumukumu
Keaha
Koke'e State Park
Kapa'a
Polihale State Park
Barking Sands Beach
Waupouli
'Opaeka'a Falls
Wailua
Waimea Canyon State Park
Wailua Falls
Wailua Bay & River
Fern Grotto
Kapaia
Hanama'ulu
Kekaha
Kokole Point
Lihu'e
Lihue Airport
Puhi
Waimea
Old Russian Fort
Niumalu
Kalapaki Bay
Kipu
Nawiliwili Harbor
Pakala
Kalaheo
Oma'o
Kaumakani
Ele'ele
Lawa'i
Hanapepe
Numila
Koloa
Hanapepe Bay
Port Allen
Poi'pu
Port Allen Airport
Kukuiula Harbor

Kaua'i
O'ahu
Ni'ihau
Moloka'i
Lana'i
Maui
Kaho'olawe
Hawai'i

● Places Of Interest
● Town Names